My First
MISSAL

My name is

....

I was born on

....

I was baptized on

....

I made my First Communion on

....

This book was given to me by

....

Pauline
BOOKS & MEDIA

Nihil Obstat:
Rev. Msgr. Dennis F. Sheehan, STD

Imprimatur:
✠ Bernard Cardinal Law
May 11, 1994

Illustrations by Carla Cortesi

Compiled by Maria Luisa Benigni

Translated by Edmund C. Lane, SSP

Original title: *Il mio primo Messalino*

Copyright © 1990, Figlie di San Paolo, Via Paolo Uccello, 9-20148 Milan, Italy

Pauline Books & Media ISBN 0-8198-4775-5

Alba House ISBN 0-8189-0679-0

St. Pauls Publications (Australia) ISBN 1-876295-20-1

English edition copyright © 1995 by the Society of St. Paul

Printed in Korea and published in the USA and Australia by the Pauline Fathers, Brothers, and Sisters.

The Society of St. Paul and the Daughters of St. Paul are international religious congregations serving the Church with the communications media.

4 5 6 7 8 9   03 02

Pauline
BOOKS & MEDIA

The Daughters of St. Paul operate book and media centers at the following addresses. Visit, call or write the one nearest you today, or find us on the World Wide Web, www.pauline.org

CALIFORNIA
3908 Sepulveda Blvd., Culver City, CA 90230; 310-397-8676
5945 Balboa Ave., San Diego, CA 92111; 858-565-9181
46 Geary Street, San Francisco, CA 94108; 415-781-5180

FLORIDA
145 S.W. 107th Ave., Miami, FL 33174; 305-559-6715

HAWAII
1143 Bishop Street, Honolulu, HI 96813; 808-521-2731
Neighbor Islands call: 800-259-8463

ILLINOIS
172 N. Michigan Ave., Chicago, IL 60601; 312-346-4228

LOUISIANA
4403 Veterans Blvd., Metairie, LA 70006; 504-887-7631

MASSACHUSETTS
Rte. 1, 885 Providence Hwy., Dedham, MA 02026; 781-326-5385

MISSOURI
9804 Watson Rd., St. Louis, MO 63126; 314-965-3512

NEW JERSEY
561 U.S. Route 1, Wick Plaza, Edison, NJ 08817; 732-572-1200

NEW YORK
150 East 52nd Street, New York, NY 10022; 212-754-1110
78 Fort Place, Staten Island, NY 10301; 718-447-5071

OHIO
2105 Ontario Street (at Prospect Ave.), Cleveland, OH 44115; 216-621-9427

PENNSYLVANIA
9171-A Roosevelt Blvd., Philadelphia, PA 19114; 215-676-9494

SOUTH CAROLINA
243 King Street, Charleston, SC 29401; 843-577-0175

TENNESSEE
4811 Poplar Ave., Memphis, TN 38117 901-761-2987

TEXAS
114 Main Plaza, San Antonio, TX 78205; 210-224-8101

VIRGINIA
1025 King Street, Alexandria, VA 22314; 703-549-3806

CANADA
3022 Dufferin Street, Toronto, Ontario, Canada M6B 3T5; 416-781-9131
1155 Yonge Street, Toronto, Ontario, Canada M4T 1W2; 416-934-3440

¡También somos su fuente para libros, videos y música en español!

Contents

IT'S SUNDAY, THE LORD'S DAY!

It's Sunday!

Let's rejoice because GOD THE FATHER
has made everything that is.

Let's rejoice because JESUS CHRIST
has risen from the dead.

Let's rejoice because the HOLY SPIRIT
makes us one in love.

In the name of the FATHER, and of the SON,
and of the HOLY SPIRIT,
together, young and old,
let us celebrate the EUCHARIST.

This is the day the Lord has made!

WE CELEBRATE
THE EUCHARIST

COME

Introductory Rites

Entrance Song

While the priest comes in, we sing a song that shows how happy we are to be able to be part of this celebration.

The Priest Greets Us

Priest: In the name of the Father, and of the Son, and of the Holy Spirit.

People: Amen.

Priest: The grace of our Lord Jesus Christ
and the love of God
and the fellowship of the Holy Spirit
be with you all.

People: And also with you.

We Ask for Forgiveness

Priest: My brothers and sisters,
to prepare ourselves to celebrate the sacred
mysteries, let us call to mind our sins.

*After thinking about what wrong things we have done,
we all say together:*

**People: I confess to almighty God,
and to you, my brothers and sisters,
that I have sinned through my own fault
in my thoughts and in my words,
in what I have done,
and in what I have failed to do;
and I ask blessed Mary, ever virgin,
all the angels and saints,
and you, my brothers and sisters,
to pray for me to the Lord our God.**

(Sometimes we might say another prayer instead.)

Priest: May almighty God have mercy on
us, forgive us our sins,
and bring us to everlasting life.

***People*: Amen.**

Invocations

Priest: Lord, have mercy.
People: Lord, have mercy.

Priest: Christ, have mercy.
People: Christ, have mercy.

Priest: Lord, have mercy.
People: Lord, have mercy.

11

GLORIA

We Pray and Thank God the Father

This is a song that praises God. It is said or sung on feast days and on all Sundays except during Lent and Advent.

People: **Glory to God in the highest,**
　　　　and peace to his people on earth.
　　　Lord God, heavenly King,
　　　almighty God and Father,
　　　　we worship you, we give you thanks,
　　　　we praise you for your glory.
　　　Lord Jesus Christ, only Son of the Father,
　　　Lord God, Lamb of God,
　　　you take away the sin of the world:
　　　　have mercy on us;
　　　you are seated at the right hand of the
　　　　　Father:
　　　　receive our prayer.

**For you alone are the Holy One,
you alone are the Lord,
you alone are the Most High,
  Jesus Christ,
  with the Holy Spirit,
  in the glory of God the Father. Amen.**

After this hymn, the priest says a prayer that tells us what today's celebration is about. At the end of the prayer, we answer:

***People:* Amen.**

13

LISTENING

The Liturgy of the Word

When we love someone, we enjoy listening to what that person has to say. The Bible tells us what God has done for our human family since time began. This is why we want to listen to the reading. It is God speaking to us today.

The First Reading

Most of the time this reading is taken from the Old Testament, that part of the Bible that tells us what God did and said before the coming of Jesus.

The reader ends by saying:

The word of the Lord.

We answer:

Thanks be to God.

The Second Reading

This reading is taken from the letters that the Apostles wrote to the very first Christians, and so also to us.

The reader ends by saying:
The word of the Lord.

We answer:
Thanks be to God.

The Gospel

*We stand up to sing the Alleluia and to get ready
to listen to the gospel.*

Deacon (or Priest): The Lord be with you.

People: And also with you.

Deacon (or Priest): A reading from the holy gospel
        according to....

People: Glory to you, Lord.

After reading the gospel, the deacon (or priest) says:
The gospel of the Lord.

We answer:
Praise to you, Lord Jesus Christ.

The Homily

*We sit down to listen to the priest. He invites and
encourages us to live according to the teachings we
have heard in the Word of God.*

PROFESSION OF FAITH

The Creed is a prayer that goes back to the early days of the Church. In this prayer we express our faith. This means that we say what we believe about God and about the Church. Our parents and godparents professed this faith for us on the day of our Baptism.

(Sometimes, instead of this Creed, the priest might have us pray the Apostles' Creed.)

People: **We believe in one God,**
       the Father, the Almighty,
       maker of heaven and earth,
       of all that is seen and unseen.

We believe in one Lord, Jesus Christ,
  the only Son of God,
  eternally begotten of the Father,
  God from God, Light from Light,
  true God from true God,
  begotten, not made, one in Being
    with the Father.
  Through him all things were made.

18

For us men and for our salvation
   he came down from heaven:
by the power of the Holy Spirit
   he was born of the Virgin Mary,
      and became man.
For our sake he was crucified under
      Pontius Pilate;
   he suffered, died, and was buried.
   On the third day he rose again
      in fulfillment of the Scriptures;
   he ascended into heaven
      and is seated at the right hand of
         the Father.
He will come again in glory to judge
      the living and the dead,
   and his kingdom will have no end.

We believe in the Holy Spirit, the Lord,
the giver of life,
who proceeds from the Father and the
Son.
With the Father and the Son he is
worshiped and glorified.
He has spoken through the Prophets.

We believe in one holy catholic and
apostolic Church.
We acknowledge one baptism for the
forgiveness of sins.
We look for the resurrection of the
dead,
and the life of the world to come.
Amen.

The General Intercessions
(Prayer of the Faithful)

*Now we pray for the needs of the world, the Church,
our country and our community.*

To each short prayer we answer:

People: **Lord, hear our prayer.**

GIVING THANKS

The Liturgy of the Eucharist

This is the second part of the Mass. The priest thanks God for all the wonderful things in the world and especially for the gift of his Son Jesus. In this part of the Mass the priest will recall the words and actions of Jesus at the Last Supper. The bread and wine will become Jesus' Body and Blood.

The Presentation of the Gifts

Bread and wine are brought to the altar.

Money and perhaps some things needed by the church and the poor are also collected.

Before placing the bread on the altar,
the priest may say:

Priest: Blessed are you, Lord, God of all creation.
Through your goodness we have this bread
to offer,
which earth has given and human hands
have made.
It will become for us the bread of life.

People: **Blessed be God for ever.**

Before placing the chalice (cup) of wine on the altar,
the priest may say:

Priest: Blessed are you, Lord, God of all creation.
Through your goodness we have this wine
to offer,
fruit of the vine and work of human hands.
It will become our spiritual drink.

People: **Blessed be God for ever.**

Invitation to Prayer

The priest asks God to accept our gifts.

Priest: Pray, brethren, that our sacrifice
       may be acceptable to God, the almighty
       Father.

**People: May the Lord accept the sacrifice at
       your hands
       for the praise and glory of his name,
       for our good, and the good of all his
       Church.**

*The priest says a special prayer for today's Mass. At
the end, we all answer:*

People: Amen.

EUCHARISTIC PRAYER III

We Praise and Thank God for All the Beautiful Things in Our Life

Priest: The Lord be with you.
People: **And also with you.**
Priest: Lift up your hearts.
People: **We lift them up to the Lord.**
Priest: Let us give thanks to the Lord our God.
People: **It is right to give him thanks and praise.**

The priest now offers a prayer similar to this one:

Priest: Father, all powerful and ever-living God,
we do well always and everywhere to give
you thanks.

In you we live and move and have our
being.
Each day you show us a Father's love;
your Holy Spirit, dwelling within us,
gives us on earth the hope of unending joy.

24

Your gift of the Spirit,
who raised Jesus from the dead,
is the foretaste and promise
of the paschal feast of heaven.
With thankful praise,
in company with the angels,
we glorify the wonders of your power:

People: **Holy, holy, holy Lord, God of power
and might,
heaven and earth are full of your glory.
Hosanna in the highest.
Blessed is he who comes in the name of
the Lord.
Hosanna in the highest.**

We Praise God and Ask Him
to Accept Our Offering

Priest: Father, you are holy indeed,
and all creation rightly gives you praise.
All life, all holiness comes from you
through your Son, Jesus Christ our Lord,
by the working of the Holy Spirit.
From age to age you gather a people to
yourself,
so that from east to west
a perfect offering may be made
to the glory of your name.

And so, Father, we bring you these gifts.
We ask you to make them holy by the
power of your Spirit,
that they may become the body and blood
of your Son, our Lord Jesus Christ,
at whose command we celebrate this
eucharist.

Our Offering Becomes
the Body and Blood of Christ

Priest: On the night he was betrayed,
he took bread and gave you thanks and
praise.
He broke the bread, gave it to his disciples
and said:

TAKE THIS,
ALL OF YOU,
AND EAT IT:
THIS IS MY BODY
WHICH WILL BE GIVEN
UP FOR YOU.

When supper was ended, he took the cup.
Again he gave you thanks and praise,
gave the cup to his disciples, and said:

**TAKE THIS,
ALL OF YOU,
AND DRINK FROM IT:
THIS IS THE CUP OF MY BLOOD,
THE BLOOD OF THE NEW
AND EVERLASTING COVENANT.
IT WILL BE SHED
FOR YOU AND FOR ALL
SO THAT SINS MAY BE FORGIVEN.
DO THIS IN MEMORY OF ME.**

Priest: Let us proclaim the mystery of faith.

People: **Christ has died, Christ is risen, Christ
will come again.**

(Another prayer may also be used.)

28

We Pray for One Another

Priest: Father, calling to mind the death your Son
endured for our salvation,
his glorious resurrection and ascension into
heaven,
and ready to greet him when he comes
again,
we offer you in thanksgiving this holy and
living sacrifice.

Look with favor on your Church's offering,
and see the Victim whose death has
reconciled us to yourself.
Grant that we, who are nourished by his
body and blood,
may be filled with his Holy Spirit,
and become one body, one spirit in Christ.

May he make us an everlasting gift to you
and enable us to share in the inheritance of
your saints,
with Mary, the virgin Mother of God;
with the apostles, the martyrs (Saint N.),
and all your saints,
on whose constant intercession we rely for
help.

We Pray for God's Family

Priest: Lord, may this sacrifice,
which has made our peace with you,
advance the peace and salvation of all the
world.
Strengthen in faith and love your pilgrim
Church on earth;
your servant, Pope N., our bishop N.,
and all the bishops,
with the clergy and the entire people your
Son has gained for you.
Father, hear the prayers of the family you
have gathered here before you.
In mercy and love unite all your children
wherever they may be.
Welcome into your kingdom our departed
brothers and sisters,
and all who have left this world in your
friendship.
We hope to enjoy for ever the vision of
your glory,
through Christ our Lord, from whom all
good things come.

We Give Glory and Praise to God

Priest: Through him, with him, in him, in the unity
of the Holy Spirit,
all glory and honor is yours, almighty
Father, for ever and ever.

People: **Amen.**

31

COMMUNION RITE

When we're invited to a party, we sing and we talk to one another. Then we eat what was prepared for us. God, our Father, has invited us to eat the bread of life, the Body and Blood of Jesus.

Priest: Let us pray with confidence to the Father in the words our Savior gave us.

People: **Our Father, who art in heaven,**
hallowed be thy name;
thy kingdom come;
thy will be done on earth, as it is
in heaven.
Give us this day our daily bread;
and forgive us our trespasses
as we forgive those who trespass
against us;
and lead us not into temptation,
but deliver us from evil.

Priest: Deliver us, Lord, from every evil,
and grant us peace in our day.
In your mercy keep us free from sin
and protect us from all anxiety
as we wait in joyful hope
for the coming of our Savior, Jesus Christ.

People: **For the kingdom, the power and the
glory are yours, now and for ever.**

THE SIGN OF PEACE

We Pray for Peace

Priest: Lord Jesus Christ, you said to your
　　　　 apostles:
　　　　 I leave you peace, my peace I give you.
　　　　 Look not on our sins, but on the faith of
　　　　　 your Church,
　　　　 and grant us the peace and unity of your
　　　　　 kingdom
　　　　 where you live for ever and ever.

People: **Amen.**

Priest: The peace of the Lord be with you always.

People: **And also with you.**

Priest: Let us offer each other the sign of peace.

*We give the peace of Jesus to each other with a hand-
shake or a hug or some other sign. In this way we
promise to love one another, to forgive one another
and to bring God's peace with us, to our home, our
school and wherever we go.*

The Breaking of the Bread

The priest breaks the bread as Jesus did at the Last Supper. Meanwhile we sing or say:

People: **Lamb of God, you take away the sins of the world:**

have mercy on us.

Lamb of God, you take away the sins of the world:

have mercy on us.

Lamb of God, you take away the sins of the world:

grant us peace.

The altar is like a table that has been set. The Supper of the Lord is ready and we are all invited. Jesus said: "I am the bread come down from heaven. If anyone eats this bread he will live for ever." This special meal is a promise of the banquet that awaits us in heaven, where we will celebrate for ever.

> *Priest:* This is the Lamb of God
> who takes away the sins of the
> world.
> Happy are those who are called to
> his supper.

> ***People:* Lord, I am not worthy to receive you,**
> **but only say the word and I shall be healed.**

When we go up to receive communion, we express our faith again.

The priest or eucharistic minister offers me the host and says, "The body of Christ."

***I answer:* "Amen."**

Then I receive the host on my tongue or in my hand.

At some Masses we can also receive the blood of Jesus Christ from the chalice. Jesus is there under the appearance of wine.

The priest or eucharistic minister offers me the chalice and says, "The blood of Christ."

I answer: "Amen."

Then I take a sip from the chalice.

We Pray that Jesus within Us Will Give Us the Strength to Love

After communion we keep still or sing a hymn of thanksgiving. We think about Jesus, who is in us, and we talk to him as our friend. We can tell him:

Lord Jesus,
I thank you for the gift which you have given me.
Help me to be good, obedient, and generous.
I pray for my parents,
my brothers and sisters, and my friends.
I also pray for the Pope
and for everybody who tries to do good for others.
I want everyone to know and love you.
I want to live in a way that pleases you.
Stay with me always, Lord Jesus.
I love you.

The priest says the prayer after communion. At the end of it, we all answer: **Amen.**

DISMISSAL

Concluding Rite

The Priest Blesses Us in God's Name

Priest: The Lord be with you.

People: And also with you.

Priest: May almighty God bless you,
the Father, and the Son, and the Holy Spirit.

People: Amen.

Priest: The Mass is ended, go in peace.

People: Thanks be to God.

After a party, before leaving, we say "thank you" to whoever has invited us. In the same way at the end of our celebration we may say "thank you" to God with a song. Then we go out to bring to others the love that we've received from God.

WHEN I GO TO CHURCH

Jesus is present in every host that was conse-
crated at the Mass. The hosts that were left over
are placed in the tabernacle to be taken later to
the sick and to also be adored by us who believe
in Jesus. A small light is always burning near the
tabernacle to remind us that the Eucharist is
Jesus, really and truly alive and present.

*During the day try to find a minute to visit Jesus. You
can talk to him about the things that are important to
you. Then listen in silence. Sometimes he will speak in
your heart. You might use these words to pray to Jesus:*

Jesus, I believe that you are here,
that you watch over me
and listen to my prayers.
You are my very best friend.
You are always close to me,
and to everyone who wants to
    love and obey you.
But you are also close to those
    who want to live without you.
You love them too, and you want
    us to pray for them.

Even though I cannot see you, I believe that you
  are with me.
Help me to love everyone I meet
and to notice people who need help.
I pray for all who are suffering.
I pray for all who are sick
  and have problems.
I thank you for everything
  you have given me.
Help me to share
  with others, Jesus.
Amen.

It is an important duty to take part in the celebration of Mass every Sunday (or Saturday evening).
God our Father asks us to love him and to live as
his friends at home, at school and at play.

It is not always easy to live in a way that pleases
God. And so we need to receive communion
often and to ask God's forgiveness for our sins.
This is the only way we can be strong enough to
live the most important commandment Jesus
gave us: "Love one another as I have loved you."

THE SACRAMENT OF RECONCILIATION

There are many ways in which we admit that we have done wrong and ask forgiveness of God and of others. But the greatest way that brings us the forgiveness of God and others is the sacrament of penance or reconciliation.

Celebrate the sacrament of reconciliation by first of all recognizing the great love that God has for you. Thank him for the gift of life, for the love of your parents, relatives and friends. You might want to pray using these words:

Your Love Is Boundless, O Lord

I praise you, Lord,
with everything that I am and everything that I do.
I praise your holy name.
I remember all the wonderful things you do for me.
You are so merciful and kind.
When I do something wrong,
you do not get angry with me.
You forgive me.
You help me
to do better next time.

Your kindness is so great
   to those who love you, Lord.
It is as great as the space
   that separates the earth
from the heavens.
Let everything he has created
   praise the Lord.
I praise you, Lord.

Based on Psalm 103

My Examination of Conscience

*Now think about your life. See how you have obeyed
the Ten Commandments, the laws that God gave to
Moses. Jesus summed up the Ten Commandments in
his law of love.*

1.   I am the Lord your God: you shall not have
        strange gods before me.

        Each morning and evening do I remember
        to pray to God who loves me? Do I thank
        him for all the good things he has done for
        me?

2. You shall not take the name of the Lord,
    your God, in vain.

    Have I used God's name or the name of
    Jesus in the wrong way, in joking around or
    when I was angry?

3. Remember to keep holy the Lord's day.

    Have I gone to Mass on Sundays (or Satur-
    day evenings) each week? Do I go to all of
    my religion classes? Do I help others to
    celebrate at Mass by smiling and being
    happy?

4. Honor your father and your mother.

    Do I sometimes talk back to my parents?
    Have I done what they told me to do? Do I
    listen to their advice? Do I help out around
    the house?

5. You shall not kill.

    Have I been angry with others?
    Have I wanted to hurt them in some way?
    Have I fought with my brothers and sisters?
    Have I hurt anybody on purpose?

6. You shall not commit adultery.

    Do I treat my body and everyone else's

body with respect? Do I avoid talking about things that might cause me to do something I shouldn't? Do I look only at pictures and watch TV shows and videos that are good?

7.   You shall not steal.

Have I taken anything that did not belong to me? Have I returned things which I borrowed?

8.   You shall not bear false witness.

Do I always tell the truth, even when it may be hard? When I have done something wrong, do I admit it? Have I lied about others?

9.   You shall not covet your neighbor's wife.

Am I jealous when someone I like likes somebody else? Am I envious of the friends of others?

10.   You shall not covet your neighbor's goods.

Do I wish I had what belongs to someone else? Am I happy to see others happy? Do I mind helping people who are poor?

After seeing how you have kept God's Ten Commandments, you might like to say this prayer:

Accept Us, O Lord

We praise you, Lord.
You are the God of our fathers.
You, more than anyone else,
    are worthy to be praised
    and glorified forever.
We admit that we have done
    things that were wrong.
We have sinned against you
    and have not loved you as we should.
We have not always obeyed the commandments
which you gave us for our own good.
Please be merciful to us, Lord.
We promise to do better and to follow you with all
    our heart.
We do not want to offend you again.
We want to be close to you.
Treat us with kindness and compassion.
Save us with your wonderful power, O Lord.
Give glory to your name.

Based on "The Canticle of Azariah" from Chapter 3 of the Book of Daniel

My Confession

The priest represents Jesus and the Church. When you go to confess your sins he will welcome you and listen to you as a good father.

Priest: In the name of the Father and of the Son and of the Holy Spirit.

***I answer:* Amen.**

Priest: May the grace of the Holy Spirit
fill your heart with light,
that you may confess your sins with loving trust
and come to know that God is merciful.

(The priest may use different words to greet you.)

Next the priest may read from the Bible about how good God is and how ready he is to forgive.

Tell the priest your sins as honestly as you can. Accept the prayers or good deeds that he gives you as a penance. This shows that you want to live a new life.

The priest will then ask you to tell God you are sorry for your sins. You can use these words (or others like them):

My God, I am sorry for my sins
with all my heart.
In choosing to do wrong
and failing to do good,
I have sinned against you
whom I should love above all things.
I firmly intend, with your help,
to do penance, to sin no more,
and to avoid whatever leads me to sin.
Our Savior Jesus Christ
suffered and died for us.
In his name, my God, have mercy.

Or:

Lord Jesus, Son of God,
have mercy on me, a sinner.

After you say your prayer of sorrow,
the priest will recite these words of
forgiveness in the name of Jesus:

Priest: God, the Father of
mercies,
through the death and
resurrection of his Son
has reconciled the
world to himself
and sent the Holy Spirit

among us
for the forgiveness of sins;
through the ministry of the Church
may God give you pardon and peace,
and I absolve you from your sins
in the name of the Father, and of the Son,
and of the Holy Spirit.

I answer: **Amen.**

Priest: Give thanks to the Lord for he is good.

I answer: **His mercy endures forever.**

The priest may then say, "The Lord has freed you from your sins. Go in peace," or other words like these.

After Confession

Try to remember that...

There is joy in heaven when one sinner on earth is sorry.

There is joy when Christians celebrate God's forgiveness.

There is joy when we, who have known God's goodness, take his peace out to the whole world.

Take some time to thank God and ask him to help you keep your promises to be better. You might like to use this prayer:

I thank you Lord, for having forgiven me

I praise you Lord.
With all the love that is in me I praise your holy
    name.
You forgive all my sins, Lord,
and you heal all my weakness.
You bless me with love and compassion.

You make me feel strong and happy—
just like an eagle flying high in the sky.
You don't treat me according to the mistakes
    I've made.
You don't repay me for my sins.
Your love for me, Lord, will last for ever.

Based on Psalm 103

52